Homeland Security Officer

Careers with Character

Career Assessments & Their Meaning
Childcare Worker
Clergy
Computer Programmer
Financial Advisor
Firefighter
Homeland Security Officer
Journalist
Manager
Military & Elite Forces Officer
Nurse
Politician
Professional Athlete & Sports Official
Psychologist
Research Scientist
Social Worker
Special Education Teacher
Veterinarian

CAREERS WITH CHARACTER

Homeland Security Officer

Ellyn Sanna

Mason Crest

Mason Crest
450 Parkway Drive, Suite D
Broomall, PA 19008
www.masoncrest.com

Printed in the Hashemite Kingdom of Jordan.

First printing
9 8 7 6 5 4 3 2 1

Series ISBN: 978-1-4222-2750-3
ISBN: 978-1-4222-2757-2
ebook ISBN: 978-1-4222-9053-8

The Library of Congress has cataloged the
hardcopy format(s) as follows:

Library of Congress Cataloging-in-Publication Data

Sanna, Ellyn, 1957-
Homeland security officer / Ellyn Sanna.
pages cm - (Careers with character)
Audience: Grade 7 to 8.
Includes index.
ISBN 978-1-4222-2757-2 (hardcover) - ISBN 978-1-4222-2750-3 (series) - ISBN 978-1-4222-9053-8 (ebook)
1. Police–United States–Juvenile literature. 2. Law enforcement–United States–Juvenile literature. 3. Law enforcement–Vocational guidance–United States–Juvenile literature. I. Title.
HV8138.S27 2014
363.2023–dc23

2013007509

Produced by Vestal Creative Services.
www.vestalcreative.com

Photo Credits:
Comstock: pp. 33, 74
Corbis: pp. 60, 62, 63
Corel: pp. 10, 17, 29, 36, 79, 82
Krasimir Kanev | Dreamstime.com: p. 70
PhotoDisc: pp. 13, 14, 18, 26, 28, 30, 38, 39, 42, 44, 45, 46, 47, 48, 49, 52, 54, 55, 66, 68, 71, 77, 78, 84, 88

The individuals in these images are models, and the images are for illustrative purposes only. To the best knowledge of the publisher, all other images are in the public domain. If any image has been inadvertantly uncredited or miscredited, please notify Vestal Creative Services, Vestal, New York 13850, so that rectification can be made for future printings.

CONTENTS

We each leave a fingerprint on the world.
Our careers are the work we do in life.
Our characters are shaped by the choices
we make to do good.
When we combine careers with character,
we touch the world with power.

INTRODUCTION

by Dr. Cheryl Gholar
and Dr. Ernestine G. Riggs

In today's world, the awesome task of choosing or staying in a career has become more involved than one would ever have imagined in past decades. Whether the job market is robust or the demand for workers is sluggish, the need for top-performing employees with good character remains a priority on most employers' lists of "must have" or "must keep." When critical decisions are being made regarding a company or organization's growth or future, job performance and work ethic are often the determining factors as to who will remain employed and who will not.

How does one achieve success in one's career and in life? Victor Frankl, the Austrian psychologist, summarized the concept of success in the preface to his book *Man's Search for Meaning* as: "The unintended side-effect of one's personal dedication to a course greater than oneself." Achieving value by responding to life and careers from higher levels of knowing and being is a specific goal of teaching and learning in "Careers with Character." What constitutes success for us as individuals can be found deep within our belief system. Seeking, preparing, and attaining an excellent career that aligns with our personality is an outstanding goal. However, an excellent career augmented by exemplary character is a visible expression of the human need to bring meaning, purpose, and value to our work.

Career education informs us of employment opportunities, occupational outlooks, earnings, and preparation needed to perform certain tasks. Character education provides insight into how a person of good character might choose to respond, initiate an action, or perform specific tasks in the presence of an ethical dilemma. "Careers with Character" combines the two and teaches students that careers are more than just jobs. Career development is incomplete without character development. What better way to explore careers and character than to make them a single package to be opened, examined, and reflected upon as a means of understanding the greater whole of who we are and what work can mean when one chooses to become an employee of character?

Character can be defined simply as "who you are even when no one else is around." Your character is revealed by your choices and actions. These bear your personal signature, validating the story of who you are. They are the fingerprints you leave behind on the people you meet and know; they are the ideas you bring into reality. Your choices tell the world what you truly believe.

Character, when viewed as a standard of excellence, reminds us to ask ourselves when choosing a career: "Why this particular career, for what purpose, and to what end?" The authors of "Careers with Character" knowledgeably and passionately, through their various vignettes, enable one to experience an inner journey that is both intellectual and moral. Students will find themselves, when confronting decisions in real life, more prepared, having had experiential learning opportunities through this series. The books, however, do not separate or negate the individual good from the academic skills or intellect needed to perform the required tasks that lead to productive career development and personal fulfillment.

Each book is replete with exemplary role models, practical strategies, instructional tools, and applications. In each volume, individuals of character work toward ethical leadership, learning how to respond appropriately to issues of not only right versus wrong, but issues of right versus right, understanding the possible benefits and consequences of their decisions. A wealth of examples is provided.

What is it about a career that moves our hearts and minds toward fulfilling a dream? It is our character. The truest approach to finding out who we are and what illuminates our lives is to look within. At the very heart of career development is good character. At the heart of good character is an individual who knows and loves the good, and seeks to share the good with others. By exploring careers and character together, we create internal and external environments that support and enhance each other, challenging students to lead conscious lives of personal quality and true richness every day.

Is there a difference between doing the right thing, and doing things right? Career questions ask, "What do you know about a specific career?" Character questions ask, "Now that you know about a specific career, what will you choose to do with what you know?" "How will you perform certain tasks and services for others, even when no one else is around?" "Will all individuals be given your best regardless of their socioeconomic background, physical condition, ethnicity, or religious beliefs?" Character questions often challenge the authenticity of what we say we believe and value in the workplace and in our personal lives.

Character and career questions together challenge us to pay attention to our lives and not fall asleep on the job. Career knowledge, self-knowledge, and ethical wisdom help us answer deeper questions about the meaning of work; they give us permission to transform our lives. Personal integrity is the price of admission.

The insight of one "ordinary" individual can make a difference in the world—if that one individual believes that character is an amazing gift to uncap knowledge and talents to empower the human community. Our world needs everyday heroes in the workplace—and "Careers with Character" challenges students to become those heroes.

A good character is an essential job requirement for a homeland security officer.

JOB REQUIREMENTS

Considering career options is one way to get yourself ready for the future . . . and choosing to be a person of character is another.

CHAPTER ONE

Something thudded in the dark. Maggie Brown froze, and eased herself higher in the front seat of the car, her hand hovering automatically over her gun. Cautiously, she peered out her window at the dark house she and her partner had been watching all night.

"Nothing." Jack Pucinelli sighed, his voice heavy with disappointment. "It's just a dog prowling around the garbage cans."

Maggie relaxed back into her seat. The police department had gotten a tip that a drug deal was going down at this address sometime tonight, but the stakeout had lasted hours with no sign of action. She wondered if their source had led them astray—or if the dealers who were said to do business at this address had gotten a tip of their own warning them to cancel tonight's deal. Either way, she and Jack would stay here until their shift ended, just to be sure they didn't miss anything.

Part of her was as disappointed as her partner was. Another part of her, though, was relieved to have a quiet night where she was not asked to make any of the tough *ethical* decisions she sometimes faced during an arrest. Maggie enjoyed her job. She loved having the power to fight for law and order. But she was also always aware that with a gun in her hand, a fine line separated her from the "bad guys." That was a line she never wanted to cross. She knew people were counting on her.

Police agencies are usually organized into geographic districts. Each officer is assigned a specific area to patrol, such as a business district or an outlying residential neighborhood. This area is the officer's "beat."

Officers need to be thoroughly familiar with their patrol area, so that they can spot anything unusual. They report or investigate suspicious circumstances and hazards to public safety.

All of us depend on officers like Maggie to keep our lives and property safe; we expect them to do so while maintaining upstanding moral characters. Homeland security officers protect us all . . . and they do so in a variety of ways, through various agencies.

Uniformed Police Officers

When you think of homeland security, police officers in uniforms may be the professionals you think of first. They work in city police departments, in small communities, and in rural areas, enforcing the law. These officers don't only work with criminals. Instead, they play an important part in the smooth functioning of their communities. Their work may range from directing traffic at the scene of a fire to investigating a burglary to giving first aid to the victim of a car accident. In some city police departments, officers are involved in community policing; this means they build relationships with the citizens of local neighborhoods and mobilize the public to help fight crime.

Sheriffs and Deputy Sheriffs

Hawaii is the only U.S. state that has no state law enforcement agency.

Sheriffs enforce the law on a county level. They are usually elected to their positions, and their departments tend to be small; most have fewer than 25 deputies. A deputy sheriff in a large agency will have

State troopers are often the first on the scene after an accident.

a job description similar to that of other police officers in city police departments.

Special Police Agencies

These agencies serve public colleges and universities, public schools, and transportation systems. In the United States, there are more than 1,300 of these agencies.

State Troopers

Troopers (sometimes called highway patrol officers) are probably best known for issuing traffic tickets to motorists who break the speed limit. They also arrest criminals statewide and patrol highways to enforce other motor vehicle

A police officer may not be a welcome sight if you've been speeding!

laws and regulations. At the scene of an accident, they direct traffic, provide first aid, and call for emergency equipment. They also provide the official report of the cause of accidents. Other law enforcement agencies, especially those in rural areas or small towns, often call on the state police for help.

Detectives

Detectives do not wear uniforms as they gather facts and collect evidence for criminal cases. Some work with interagency task forces to fight specific types of crime, and all usually specialize in one area of violation (such as homicide, fraud, or narcotics). They interview witnesses and suspects, examine records and other evidence, observe the activities of suspects, and take part in raids and arrests. They are assigned cases on a rotating basis, and they work on them until an arrest or conviction occurs—or the case is dropped.

Canadian Police Officers

The officers that protect Canada's homeland can be broken down into these three categories:

- local police services
- provincial police services (in Ontario and Quebec only)
- Royal Canadian Mounted Police (Canada's national police service)

FBI Agents

The U.S. Department of Justice is the largest employer of federal homeland security officers, and the Federal Bureau of Investigation is the U.S. government's principle law enforcement agency. These officers are responsible for investigating violations of more than 260 statutes and conducting sensitive national security investigations. Their job duties are varied: for instance, they monitor court-

You may be able to combine some of your other interests with a career as homeland security officer. For instance, are you interested in chemistry or other sciences? Do you love working with dogs or horses? Do you enjoy boating? Would you like an outdoor job? Or does the legal system fascinate you?

As a homeland security officer, professionals can choose from a wide range of special interests and working environments. For instance, some officers specialize in chemical and microscopic analysis, training and firearms instruction, or handwriting and fingerprint analysis. Others work in special units such as horseback, bicycle, motorcycle, or harbor patrol; canine corps; special weapons and tactics (SWAT) teams, or emergency response teams. Some work in jails or in courthouses.

authorized *wiretaps*, investigate *white-collar crime*, examine business records, track stolen property as it moves across state lines, collect evidence of espionage, and participate in undercover investigations. The FBI's jurisdiction covers organized crime, public corruption, financial crime, fraud against the government, bribery, *copyright infringement*, civil rights violations, bank robbery, *extortion*, kidnapping, air piracy, terrorism, espionage, interstate criminal activity, *drug trafficking*, and other violations of federal laws.

DEA Agents

Agents in the U.S. Drug Enforcement Agency enforce laws relating to illegal drugs. The DEA is America's most important agency in the enforcement of federal drug laws within the United States; it also has sole responsibility for coordinating and pursuing U.S. drug investigations in other countries. These agents conduct complex criminal investigations. They do this in a variety of ways, including surveillance of criminals and undercover infiltration of illicit drug organizations.

U.S. Marshals and Deputy Marshals

These marshals protect the federal courts and ensure that the judicial system operates smoothly. They provide protection for federal justices, transport federal prisoners, protect federal witnesses, pursue and arrest federal fugitives, and manage money or other assets seized from criminals. U.S. marshals and their deputies have the widest jurisdiction of any homeland security officer, and they are involved in some degree in nearly all federal law enforcement activities.

Members of a SWAT (Special Weapons and Tactics) team are trained to handle particularly dangerous situations.

Homeland security officers have an important role along America's borders.

U.S. Citizenship and Immigration Services Agents and Inspectors

These officers help legal visitors enter the United States—and they detain and deport those that try to enter illegally. The USCIS consists of border patrol agents, immigration, inspectors, criminal investigators and immigration agents, and detention and deportation officers. Nearly half of all USCIS officers are border patrol agents, who protect America's more than 8,000 miles of international land and water boundaries. Their mission is to detect and prevent the

Since September 11, 2001, homeland security departments in both the United States and Canada took steps to improve the safety of citizens in both countries. In the United States, these measures were taken among many others:

- More than 4,000 FBI agents were deployed to investigate the September 11, 2001 crimes.
- Fifty-six joint terrorism task forces were established and nearly 100 anti-terrorism teams to coordinate the investigations and improve communication between federal and local law enforcement.
- The nation's air, land, and seaports of entry were placed on Alert Level1, ensuring a more thorough examination of people and cargo.
- About 1,600 National Guardsmen were deployed to help secure U.S. borders and more than 9,000 to guard the nation's transportation system.
- Responded to more than 8,000 cases of anthrax attacks or hoaxes.
- Disaster Medical Assistance Teams were created to aid thousands of rescue workers.
- Provided 24-hour-a-day, 7-day-a-week security at 348 dams and hydroelectric power plants.
- The Patriot Readiness Center was developed to help federal retirees return to active service for their country. (More than 15,000 responded.)

smuggling and unlawful entry of foreigners into the United States; they also seize contraband, such as narcotics, that people may attempt to smuggle across the border. Another branch of the USCIS, immigration inspectors, interview and examine people who are seeking to enter the United States legally. They inspect passports and process applications for immigration or temporary residence in the United States.

ATF Agents

Special agents employed by the U.S. Department of the Treasury work for the Bureau of Alcohol, Tobacco, and Firearms. They investigate violations of federal firearm and explosive laws, as well as federal alcohol and tobacco tax regulations.

Customs Agents

These officers investigate violations of drug smuggling, *money laundering*, child pornography, customs fraud, and enforcement of the laws regulating the exportation of arms. Their investigations may be either within U.S. boundaries or outside them, and they use informants, physical and electronic surveillance techniques, and careful examination of records from importers and exporters, banks, and manufacturers. They conduct interviews, serve on task forces with other agencies, and obtain and execute search warrants.

Customs Inspectors

The job of customs inspectors is different from customs agents. These officers inspect the cargo, baggage, clothing, and packages of people who are entering or leaving the United States, whether by car, ship, train, or aircraft. Customs inspectors count, weigh, measure, and sample the cargoes entering and leaving the United States. They seize illegal or smuggled items, and they apprehend, detain, and arrest violators of U.S. laws.

Secret Service Agents

The U.S. Secret Service protects the President, Vice President, and their immediate families. They also guard the safety of presidential candidates, former presidents, and foreign dignitaries who are visiting the United States. Secret Service agents also investigate counterfeiting, forgery of government checks or bonds, and the fraudulent use of credit cards.

Bureau of Diplomatic Security Special Agents

These officers play an important role in the ongoing battle against terrorism. Overseas, they advise U.S. ambassadors on all security matters; within the United States, they investigate passport and visa fraud, conduct investigations on personnel backgrounds, issue security clearances, and protect the Secretary of State and a number of foreign dignitaries. They also train foreign civilian police and administer a reward program for counter-terrorism.

Coast Guard Officers

The Coast Guard plays an important role in U.S. homeland security. It protects ports and the marine transportation system from terrorism, and it guards U.S. waters from illegal drugs, illegal aliens, firearms, and weapons of mass destruction. In addition, Coast Guard officers protect against illegal fishing and the destruction of living marine resources by

> Police departments in some large cities hire high school graduates who are still in their teens as police cadets or trainees. These individuals will do clerical work and attend classes for one or two years. Once they reach the minimum age requirement—if they have performed satisfactorily—they are appointed to the regular police force.

working to prevent and respond to oil and other hazardous material spills.

National Guard Members

Although the National Guard is actually a part of the U.S. military, the men and women who serve in it play an important role in homeland security. They help their communities in times of emergencies such as hurricanes, floods, tornados, earthquakes, forest fires, and other national disasters. The National Guard gives men and women the opportunity to have a second career and earn additional income while serving their country on weekends and for two or more weeks a year. High school students who are 17 or older can join while they are still in school; they serve one weekend a month and a week during the summer, earning a paycheck all through their senior year of school. Many college students also serve in the National Guard, and in return they receive funds for their education.

Educational Background

Many colleges offer degrees in law enforcement—but no particular degree is required for most homeland security jobs, both in the United States and Canada. Instead, if you want to be a homeland security officer, you must meet the necessary civil service regulations. In the United States, this means you must be a U.S. citizen, at least 20 years old, and able to pass physical and personal examinations. These assessments include tests of vision, hearing, strength, and agility. Your eligibility will also depend on your performance on written examinations, as well as your previous education and experience. Most larger police departments require at least a high school diploma, and federal and state agencies usually want a college degree (although a particular major is not required). Each agency has its own requirements.

For instance, applicants for special agent jobs with the DEA must have a college degree and either one year of experience conducting criminal investigations, one year of graduate school, or at least a 2.95 grade point average in college. DEA special agents must also take part in 14 weeks of specialized training at the FBI Academy in Quantico, Virginia.

U.S. Border Patrol agents must be younger than 37 years old at the time of appointment, possess a valid driver's license, and pass a three-part examination of reasoning and language skills. The job also requires a bachelor's degree or previous work experience that demonstrates the ability to handle stressful situations, make decisions, and take charge. In other words, applicants may qualify through a combination of education and/or work experiences.

Although a particular college degree is not required, many law enforcement agencies are now encouraging applicants to take college courses in subjects related to law enforcement. More and more entry-level applicants have some college education, and a significant number are now college graduates.

Many junior colleges, colleges, and universities offer programs in law enforcement or administration of justice. Other courses you may find helpful if you're interested in these careers include accounting, finance, electrical engineering, computer science, and foreign languages. Physical education and sports are helpful in developing the competitiveness, stamina, and agility needed for many homeland security officers.

Whatever their educational backgrounds, however, before their first assignments almost all officers go through a period of training. In state and large city police departments, *recruits* are trained in the agency's police academy for a 12- to 14-week period. Smaller police departments often send their new recruits to a regional or state academy. The training will include classroom instruction on constitutional law and civil rights, state and local laws, and accident investigation. Recruits also receive training and supervised experience in patrol, traffic control, the use of firearms, self-defense, first aid, and emergency response.

The "Right Stuff"

Like Maggie Brown, the many officers involved in homeland security all work hard to keep their country safe. Their jobs require that they be physically fit—and that they have the sort of personality that allows them to work well even in the most stressful and dangerous of situations.

If you're interested in a career as a homeland security officer, you need to determine whether you have the personality needed for this type of career. Your guidance counselor or another career counselor can probably help you honestly assess yourself to determine if you have what it takes.

Few of us have much control over our personalities, those unique packages of characteristics given to us by our environments and the genetic material passed along to us by our biological parents. But each of us can determine the sort of character we want to possess. Unlike personality, character is based on individual choices; each time we make a decision to do good, we are shaping our characters.

Because good character is so necessary to this career field, senior officers carefully interview candidates for any homeland security job; all applicants' character traits and backgrounds will be investigated closely. In some agencies, psychiatrists or psychologists also interview applicants and may administer personality tests that will help assess applicants' true characters. Most candidates for these jobs must take a lie detector test, and many are asked to comply with a drug test.

Experts in character education, like Michael Josephson and Tom Lickona, stress that a good character is built on possessing certain core qualities:

- integrity and trustworthiness
- respect and compassion
- justice and fairness
- responsibility
- courage
- self-discipline and diligence
- citizenship

Homeland security officers are authorized to use their power to enforce the laws that protect us all. Unfortunately, wherever human beings have power, they must also face the temptation to misuse that power. That's why it is essential that homeland security officers do their jobs in a way that honors the character qualities listed above. In the chapters that follow, we will look at each of these character traits—and see how it is lived out in the lives of homeland security officers.

Values are the foundation of our character and of our confidence. A person who does not know what he stands for or what he should stand for will never enjoy true happiness and success.

—Lionel Kendrick

If you're going to carry a gun and wear a badge, you will also need integrity and trustworthiness.

INTEGRITY AND TRUSTWORTHINESS

Even honest people can be tempted to evade the truth.

CHAPTER TWO

Sheriff Doug Watson's mind was on other things. A year ago, his eight-year-old son had been diagnosed with a rare medical condition. Now, the doctors were saying his only chance of survival might be a new treatment—but it cost tens of thousands of dollars, and Doug's insurance would not cover the expense of medication that was still experimental. When Doug's car radio crackled to life, he listened almost absently to the report of an escaped bank robber reported to be in the area. Nothing seemed as important to him right now as his son's life.

When he spotted a vehicle matching the description he had just heard on the radio, however, his mind jerked to attention. He

Some situations a police officer encounters may be far less black and white than whether a person is breaking a speed limit or not.

pushed on his siren and nosed up behind the car; to his surprise, it pulled over obediently. A man leapt out of the ramshackle vehicle and dashed into the woods, a large bag hanging from his arm. Doug quickly radioed his deputy to join him in the chase; then he jumped out of his car and began running.

When people have integrity:

They don't tell lies.
They don't take what isn't theirs.
They don't cheat.
They can't use circumstances to their own advantage.
They don't allow others to assume something that isn't true.

When people have integrity, others can trust them.

For a few minutes, the man seemed to disappear, but Doug soon picked up his trail. Doug was in good physical condition, and he ran easily through the woods; meanwhile, the man ahead of him seemed to be

Officers may work alone in rural areas and small communities, but in large police departments they usually patrol with a partner. Being able to cooperate with others is a necessary skill if you want to be a homeland security officer.

flagging. Doug caught up with him, just as his deputy came charging up from behind. The man was hampered by the large bag he clutched, and he was apparently unarmed. He froze when Doug shouted, "Police! Stop where you are!" Doug read the man his rights and slapped handcuffs on him. While the deputy walked the man back up to the road, Doug hurried ahead to call the state police. As they waited for the troopers to arrive, Doug searched the criminal's bag and found that it held thousands of stolen dollars.

Several hours later, as Doug drove home from work, he could still hardly believe he and his deputy had caught the man so

Not every crisis involves danger and violence—instead, some may involve quiet issues of integrity.

30

Do the ends justify the means?

Some people believe that right and wrong are relative, depending on the situation. In other words, it might be wrong to tell a lie or steal in some situations—but in other cases, where some good result will be accomplished, a lie or theft might be justified.

Others believe that right and wrong are absolutes. From this perspective, it is always wrong to lie, steal, or hurt others.

What do you think?

If you were paid enough, would you be willing to bend your integrity? Do you think the ends would justify the means?

easily. They didn't see much action in their sleepy little corner of the world, and Doug knew that it was mostly sheer luck that had enabled them to turn the criminal over to the state police. The robber seemed to have been too terrified to resist; in fact, he looked almost relieved to be caught.

Doug pulled his car over to the side of the road where they had caught the man. He sat still for a while, thinking back over the day's events, and then he got out of the car and strolled down through the woods, retracing his steps from earlier that day. He found his thoughts turning once more to his son, and his stomach clenched with the now-familiar sense of fear and worry. How could he ever come up with the money he needed?

As he walked through the dead leaves beneath the trees, he caught a glimpse of something that pulled his attention away from his anxiety. In the mouth of a woodchuck hole, he could see a loop of brown leather.

The four enemies of integrity:

- self-interest (The things we want . . . the things we might be tempted to lie, steal, or cheat to get.)
- self-protection (The things we don't want . . . the things we'd lie, steal, or cheat to avoid.)
- self-deception (When we refuse to see the situation clearly.)
- self-righteousness (When we think we're always right . . . an end-justifies-the-means attitude.)

Adapted from materials from the Josephson Institute of Ethics, josephsoninstitute.org.

An *ethical dilemma* is a situation that demands we make a choice about what is the right thing to do. If we want to be people who value the qualities of good character, then we must take the time to sort out these ethical dilemmas carefully.

32

How would you feel if your actions were the headlines on today's newspaper?

One way to solve an ethical dilemma is to use this technique:

Imagine that whatever choice you make will be broadcast as the headline in a newspaper. How would you feel if the whole world knew your decision? How would you feel if your mother knew? Or if the children in your life were aware of the choice you had made?

If your answer to this question makes you feel uncomfortable, ashamed, or embarrassed, chances are you are not making a moral decision. When we choose to act with integrity, we do not need to be afraid that others will find out what we have done. We can hold our heads high, knowing we have done the right thing.

Doug pulled on the strap . . . and found himself holding a small leather bag. When he unzipped it, handfuls of hundred-dollar bills spilled out.

Hardly able to believe his eyes, Doug counted the money. After what seemed an eternity, he had counted to 507. He stared down at the green bills, realizing he was looking at more than

These lines from an ancient Indian poem "The Mahabharata" summarize Hindu views of right and wrong:

This is the sum of all righteousness: deal with others as you would yourself be dealt with. Do nothing to your neighbor which you would not want him to do to you later.

A lie told for the sake of a righteous end ceases to be a falsehood.

What do you think? Is something as intangible as integrity more important than cash?

$50,000. The robber must have stashed the money here, hoping that if he were caught, he would be able to come back later and retrieve it.

It occurred to him that the money would more than cover his son's medical treatment. Doug knew he couldn't keep the money . . . but as he slowly packed the money back into the bag, he couldn't help thinking that the entire day seemed like a dream. From beginning to end, events had seemed to fall into place as though they were meant to happen a certain way. Was it just coincidence he had been able to catch the man so easily? And was it sheer chance he had stumbled across this money? If he never said anything, no one would ever know he had found it. . . .

Doug was an honest man who never told a lie if he could help it—and he had never stolen anything in his life. He gave a shamefaced laugh as he realized what he was considering, and then he hurried back to his car, intending to report his find immediately.

But he changed his mind when he reached the car. He was tired and eager to get home to his family. Tomorrow morning would be time enough to report the money.

Somehow, though, the days slipped by, and Doug still had not said anything to anyone about the money. Meanwhile, he knew he and his wife had to make a decision soon about their son's treatment—or it would be too late.

When Doug had first considered keeping the money, he had been shocked by his own thoughts. Now, though, the more he thought about it, the more he had gotten used to the idea. After all, he wouldn't be hurting anyone. The bank's money was covered by insurance that would make up for the missing cash. And no one would ever be able to trace its disappearance to Doug. He would have to tell his wife something, of course, to explain where he had gotten the money, but maybe he could tell her that friends had loaned it to them. . . . He would think of something to say, he knew . . . or he could if he decided to actually keep the money.

Of course, Doug would never have robbed that bank himself . . . but would he be wrong to keep the money now it had fallen into his hands? Wasn't his son's life the most important priority?

Doug is facing an ethical dilemma. What do you think he should do? What would you do if you were in his place?

Integrity is the glue that holds our way of life together.

—Billy Graham

Homeland security officers must use their power with respect and compassion for others.

RESPECT AND COMPASSION

It can be hard to determine right from wrong . . . especially when our sense of compassion pulls us in a different direction from our professional responsibilities.

CHAPTER THREE

Juan Torres stared at the family huddled in the shadows of the cave. He had been tracking them all night . . . but he had expected to find the group of drug smugglers the U.S. Border Patrol had been seeking since a tip-off the day before. Instead, the first light of the new day showed this miserable group of scared individuals. One was an old woman, who reminded Juan of his own grandmother; the other woman held a young baby to her breast, while the only man in the group stood protectively in front of her, staring defiantly at Juan. A boy about eleven clung to the man's pant leg, his eyes round and frightened as he looked up at Juan.

As a Border Patrol officer, Juan's job was to apprehend and arrest people who tried to illegally slip across the U.S.-Mexican

People who value respect and compassion:

- are courteous and polite.
- are tolerant; they accept individual's differences.
- don't mistreat or make fun of anyone.
- don't use or take advantage of others.
- respect others' rights to make their own decisions.
- are sensitive to others' feelings.
- live by the Golden Rule. (They treat others the way they want to be treated.)
- help others.
- share what they have with others.
- do what they can to help those who are in trouble.
- forgive others.

Adapted from material from the Character Counts Coalition, charactercounts.org/overview/about.html.

Immigration inspectors' work falls under the umbrella of homeland security.

When many Mexicans make their homes in dumps, life across the border in the United States can look very appealing.

border. He knew people were depending on him to keep the border safe, and he prided himself on doing his job carefully and well. But as he looked at this scared and unhappy family, it was hard to believe they were much threat to America's national security.

The younger woman straightened her shoulders and stepped alongside her husband. "Please," she said in Spanish, looking straight into Juan's eyes, "let us go." She took another step closer to him and held out her hand, as though she were begging. "We have nothing in Mexico . . . no job, no money, no food. Now we don't even have a house. We have been living in the dump outside Tijuana, eating whatever we can find. But we have family in Los Angeles. My husband's father and two brothers. They have good jobs. If we can get there, they will take us in."

Juan knew what it was like for many Mexicans. Their country's economy had been through terrible times, and more than half of the population was desperately poor. His own parents still told stories

Three Foundations for Ethical Decision-Making

1. Take into account the interests and well-being of everyone concerned. (Don't do something that will help you if it will hurt another.)
2. When a character value like integrity and trustworthiness is at stake, always make the decision that will support that value. (For example, tell the truth even though it may cost you some embarrassment.)
3. Where two character values conflict (for instance, when telling the truth might hurt another person), choose the course of action that will lead to the greatest good for everyone concerned. Be sure to seek all possible alternatives, however; don't opt for dishonesty simply as the easiest and least painful way out of a difficult situation.

Adapted from materials from the Josephson Institute of Ethics, josephsoninstitute.org.

about the hard years they had endured growing up in Mexico before they immigrated to the United States.

But Juan also knew that the woman's desperate courage and dignity might merely be an act to play on his sympathies. The man and woman could even have hired strangers to act as their children and grandmother, so they would be less apt to be suspected of criminal activity. They might in fact be the very drug smugglers he had been expecting to find.

"Please," the woman begged. "Let us go."

Juan hesitated. His gut told him these people were not drug smugglers—and he was full of compassion for them. He respected the desperation, courage, and initiative that had driven them to seek help from their family in Los Angeles. But he also had a job to do. Should he listen to his heart—or should he obey his professional regulations? What was most important?

What should he do?

Careful thought about the right way to act is compassion's relative.
—Confucius

Before the fall of the Soviet government, relations between Russia and the United States were tense—and espionage was a fact of life.

JUSTICE AND FAIRNESS

Justice demands that we treat everyone fairly—whether they are our friends or our enemies.

CHAPTER FOUR

In February 2001, FBI agents possessed the justice and fairness they needed to do something that was very difficult: they arrested a colleague who was guilty of espionage against the United States.

Robert Philip Hanssen, an FBI special agent, had a long career in counterintelligence. He was well respected by his colleagues. For years, most of them would never have dreamed their fellow agent was living a double life.

Back in 1985, Hanssen was assigned to the intelligence division at the FBI field office in New York City, where he supervised a foreign *counterintelligence* squad. Sometime that year, he was apparently recruited by the Russian government to provide them with

Double agents are often able to move among their coworkers without being noticed or suspected.

information about his own country. One of his first acts of treason was to disclose to the *KGB* the identity of two Russian officials who were acting as spies for the U.S. government. When the officials were called back to Moscow, they were convicted of espionage and executed.

But Hanssen's fellow FBI agents still did not know the truth about him. In the years that followed, he was assigned to a variety of national security posts that gave him access to classified information—and he continued to pass this information along to the government of the former Soviet Union.

Hanssen used his professional expertise to protect himself from discovery. He used drop sites to pass along information and he never met face to face with the Russians; he never revealed to the Russians his true identity or where he worked; and he constantly checked FBI records to be sure suspicion had not turned his way. Motivated by the large sums of money paid to him by the Soviet government, he was clever enough to keep his activities undetected for years.

Robert Hanssen was able to drop off thousands of pages of classified material—in exchange for thousands of dollars.

People who value justice and fairness:

- treat all people the same (as much as possible).
- consider carefully before making decisions that affect others.
- don't take advantage of others' mistakes.
- cooperate with others.
- recognize the uniqueness and value of each individual.

Adapted from material from the Character Counts Coalition, charactercounts.org/overview/about.html.

Eventually, though, after the fall of the Soviet government, the FBI learned from the Russians themselves that an American spy had been passing them information. Using computer *forensic* analysis, *covert* surveillance, and court-authorized searches, FBI agents at last put together a case against Hanssen. According to the evidence, Hanssen left packages of information for the KGB more than 20 times. He also provided the KGB with over two dozen computer discs that contained additional information. In all, he gave the KGB more than 6,000 pages of classified documentary material. In exchange for these activities,

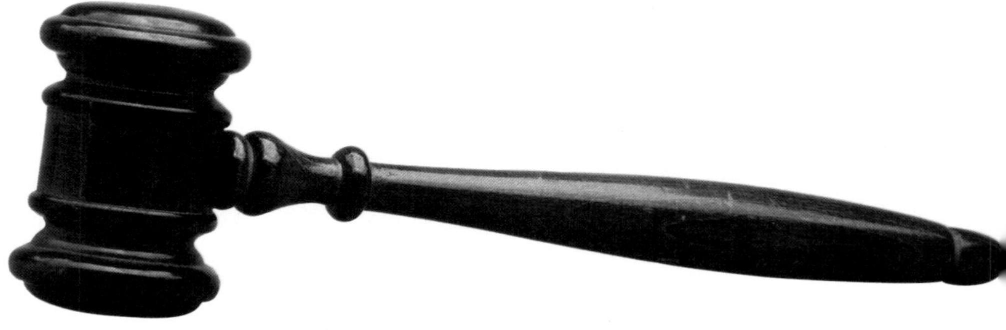

Justice is a standard that structures our culture.

What is the fair thing to do when a colleague is in the wrong? Does justice demand loyalty to the individual—or loyalty to a nation, employer, or some other higher authority?

The FBI's Core Values

According to the FBI's website, these values are essential for all FBI officers:

- rigorous obedience to the Constitution of the United States.
- uncompromising personal and institutional integrity.
- respect for the dignity of those they protect, which reminds them to use their law enforcement powers with restraint, recognizing the natural human tendency to be corrupted by power and to become callous in its exercise.
- fairness, ensuring that they treat everyone with the highest regard for constitution, civil, and human rights.

The website concludes: "We who enforce the law must not merely obey it. We have an obligation to set a moral example which those whom we protect can follow. Because the FBI's success in accomplishing its mission is directly related to the support and cooperation of those whom we protect, these core values are the fiber which holds together the vitality of our institution."

Those who enforce the law must set a moral example for others.

If you knew a friend cheated on a test, what do you think would be the fair thing to do?

he received from the Soviet government diamonds and cash worth more than $600,000.

FBI director Louis J. Freeh recognized the ethical dilemma this situation presented to Hanssen's fellow agents. They had to choose between being loyal to a colleague—and upholding justice and fairness as their guiding principle. "These kinds of cases are the most difficult . . . imaginable," he said. "I am immensely proud of the men and women of the FBI who conducted this investigation. Their actions represent counterintelligence at its very best, reflecting dedication to both principle and mission. It is not an easy assignment to investigate a colleague, but they did so unhesitatingly, quietly, and securely."

United States Attorney Helen Fahey also recognized the uncompromising fairness and justice of the FBI agents who built the case against Hanssen. "Their superlative work in this extraordinarily sensitive and important investigation," she said, "is testament to their professionalism and dedication."

If you found yourself in a situation similar to that faced by Hanssen's fellow agents, what would you do? For instance, suppose you know a friend cheated on a test . . . vandalized the school building . . . or stole something from a teacher's desk. Would you feel you should keep your friend's secret out of loyalty—or would you go to a teacher or the school principal with your knowledge?

Justice is the set and constant purpose which gives to all people their due.

—Justinian I

Sometimes the less obvious responsibilities—like taking care of our bodies—can be the most important.

RESPONSIBILITY

We can't meet our responsibilities to others if we fail to meet our responsibilities to ourselves.

CHAPTER FIVE

Dan O'Ryan worked hard at his job. As a street cop for the New York Police Department, he prided himself on being one of the most responsible officers he knew. He belonged to a special street crime unit working to get guns off the city's streets. Operation Gun-stop was a special program that gave a $1,000-reward to anyone who turned in an illegal firearm, and Dan worked long hours following up on tips the department received about gun possession. He put in lots of overtime; most weeks he worked 60 hours, and sometimes he worked even more.

People who value responsibility:

- think before they act; they consider the possible consequences of their actions.
- accept responsibility for the consequences of their choices.
- don't blame others for their mistakes or take credit for others' achievements.
- don't make excuses.
- set a good example for others.
- pursue excellence in all they do.
- do the best with what they have.
- are dependable; others can rely on them.

Adapted from material from the Character Counts Coalition, charactercounts.org/overview/about.html.

Dan was also careful to keep his own gun skills up to par. He practiced regularly at the firing range, and he signed up for seminars the department offered on self-defense. He knew people were counting on him to keep New York's streets safe, and he intended to be responsible enough to merit that trust.

Dan was almost always tired, but he had learned to ignore his body's need for sleep.

Gun control is an important part of many police officers' jobs.

People who break and enter don't keep 9-to-5 schedules!

Uniformed officers, detectives, agents, and inspectors usually work 40-hour weeks, but paid overtime is often required. Shift work is necessary in these positions because protection must be provided around the clock. (Criminals and other dangers don't keep 9 to 5 schedules.) Junior officers frequently work weekends, holidays, and nights. Police officers and detectives are required to work any time their services are needed, and they may work long hours during an ongoing investigation. In most cases, officers are expected to be armed and ready to exercise their authority to guard citizens whenever necessary, whether they are on or off duty.

In the late 19th century, women with full, curvy bodies were considered beautiful. By the early 20th century, however, thin, flat-chested women were thought to be paragons of loveliness. Physical fitness is a more important and enduring standard.

He kept his energy up by eating plenty of plump, sugary donuts at the police station, and he usually grabbed something quick and filling at his favorite "greasy spoon." His wife complained about his eating habits—but Dan just didn't have time to sit down for a salad. He needed something he could eat on the go, like pizza or hot-dogs, or even a cheeseburger from McDonald's. Of course, as the years went by, he had noticed the weight starting to stick around his

Don't confuse caring for your body responsibly with thinking you have to look a certain way. Many aspects of our culture today, such as advertising, television, movies, and magazine covers, convey the message that you have to look a certain way physically in order to be attractive.

The truth is, however, that body types are fads; they go in and out of fashion the way jean styles do. For instance, in the Renaissance, full-bodied women were considered beautiful, while in the early 20th century, thin flat-chested women were thought to be most attractive.

Healthy bodies come in all shapes and sizes. As talk show host Oprah Winfrey said, "It's not about weight—it's about caring for yourself on a daily basis."

middle—but as hard as he worked, he needed all the energy he could get; he didn't have room in his life for dieting.

Recently, though, as Dan was chasing a suspect through the streets, he could feel his heart pounding as he ran . . . and he just couldn't seem to keep up enough speed to gain on the fleeing man. In desperation, he had pulled his gun and shouted at the man to freeze. The man had kept running, though . . . and Dan had let him go. He couldn't bring himself to shoot someone in the back just because he had gotten too fat and lazy to keep up.

In the days since that incident, Dan had done a lot of thinking. He knew the department was offering a new diet and exercise program, and a few guys had signed up for it. Some of the other officers were giving them a hard time, and Dan had done his share of teasing. The program included a segment on stress and learning to release tension, and he had never cared much for anything that

Taking Care of You

It's not just your body that needs care and attention. So do your emotions. Because of the stress they face, homeland security officers of all sorts must be careful to address their emotional needs—or they will burn out.

Here are some ways to take care of yourself emotionally:

- Keep a journal where you can be honest about your feelings.
- Talk to someone when you feel upset—a close friend, a school counselor, a pastor or rabbi, or anyone you trust.
- Make time for being alone regularly and get in touch with the "real you."
- Learn and practice relaxation techniques.

smacked of psychology. He wasn't one of those guys who wanted to get in touch with his own feelings.

Now, though, he wondered if he should consider signing up for the weight-loss program.

What do you think the responsible thing would be for him to do?

59

One is responsible for one's own life.

—Madeleine Kuhn

Homeland security officers on board Coast Guard ships need courage to do their jobs well.

COURAGE

People who have courage do the right thing . . . even when they're scared.

CHAPTER SIX

Bernard Webber still remembers February 18, 1952. That was the day when, at ten to six in the morning, in the midst of rough seas, a small oil tanker called the *Pendleton* snapped in two. The bow section carried the captain and seven crewmen to their deaths. In the stern, the chief engineer took charge of the 32 survivors. Adrift amid waves like towering mountains, the broken ship drifted south about six miles off Cape Cod.

Early in the afternoon, the men at the Coast Guard Station spotted the broken pieces of the *Pendleton*. The Officer in Charge, Bos'n Cluff, turned to Bernard Webber and ordered him to pick himself a crew. Webber had seen the conditions offshore, and he

Today, the Coast Guard performs many rescues.

People who value courage:

- say what's right (even when no one agrees with them).
- do the right thing (even when it's hard).
- follow their conscience (instead of the crowd).
- keep going in spite of hardship or difficulty.
- endure danger in order to be true to the other core qualities of a good character.

was terrified. He knew he could die in the next few hours. Mustering his courage, he agreed to go.

As he chose his crew, he found that only three men were available. The rest of the men had slipped away rather than face near-certain death. According to the Naval Institute's *Proceedings*, as Webber and his crew rowed out to the rescue ship, a local fisherman shouted to them, "You guys better get lost before you get too far out." Webber understood what the man meant. He had two choices: go out to the broken ship and probably die—or pretend to get lost and live to see another day. Webber's only answer to the fisherman was to ask him to call Webber's wife and let her know what was happening.

After the terrorist attacks of September 11, 2001, the Coast Guard played an increasingly important role in homeland security. In the six months since the attacks, Coast Guard units had:

- conducted over 35,000 port security patrols.
- conducted over 3,500 air patrols.
- boarded over 10,000 vessels.
- conducted over 2,000 boardings of "high interest vessels."
- escorted 6,000 vessels in or out of port.
- conducted over 7,000 search and rescues.
- helped over 10,000 mariners.
- saved over 731 lives.
- interdicted 1,529 illegal immigrants.
- responded to 115 pollution cases.
- maintained over 124 Security Zones.
- seized 70,560 pounds of cocaine and 19,534 pounds of marijuana.

The Coast Guard uses helicopters as well as boats to keep U.S. coasts safe.

Three Foundations for Ethical Decision-Making

1. Take into account the interests and well-being of everyone concerned. (Don't do something that will help you if it will hurt another.)
2. When a character value like integrity and trustworthiness is at stake, always make the decision that will support that value. (For example, tell the truth even though it may cost you some embarrassment.)
3. Where two character values conflict (for instance, when telling the truth might hurt another person), choose the course of action that will lead to the greatest good for everyone concerned. Be sure to seek all possible alternatives, however; don't opt for dishonesty simply as the easiest and least painful way out of a difficult situation.

Adapted from materials from the Josephson Institute of Ethics, 4640 Admiralty Way, Suite 1001, Marina del Rey, California 90292.

As Webber's ship traveled out into the seas, a wave tossed it high into the air. It landed on its side, and tons of seawater crashed over the deck, breaking the windshield and compass and knocking Webber flat. The self-righting boat recovered quickly, and Webber struggled back to his feet. He fought to regain control of the boat on its roller-coaster ride through the waves. Snow lashed his face through the broken windshield, and he could barely see. He was afraid he had missed the broken ship altogether.

At last, however, he reached the stern portion of the *Pendleton*. One by one, he and his crew pulled the stranded sailors into their own ship. Now he had to get them to safety. With no compass and zero visibility, Webber knew they might all still die. But he pushed ahead.

And he made it. Thanks to the Coast Guard officer's courage in the face of death, he brought his crew as well as the *Pendleton's* back to safety.

Bernard Webber faced an ethical dilemma when his commanding officer ordered him to head out into a dangerous storm. He could have chosen to protect himself; that was the option other crewmen took, and they would have certainly understood if Webber had done the same. But Webber chose instead to act with courage.

What do you think you would have done in his place?

Never let your fears make your decisions.

—Sean Covey

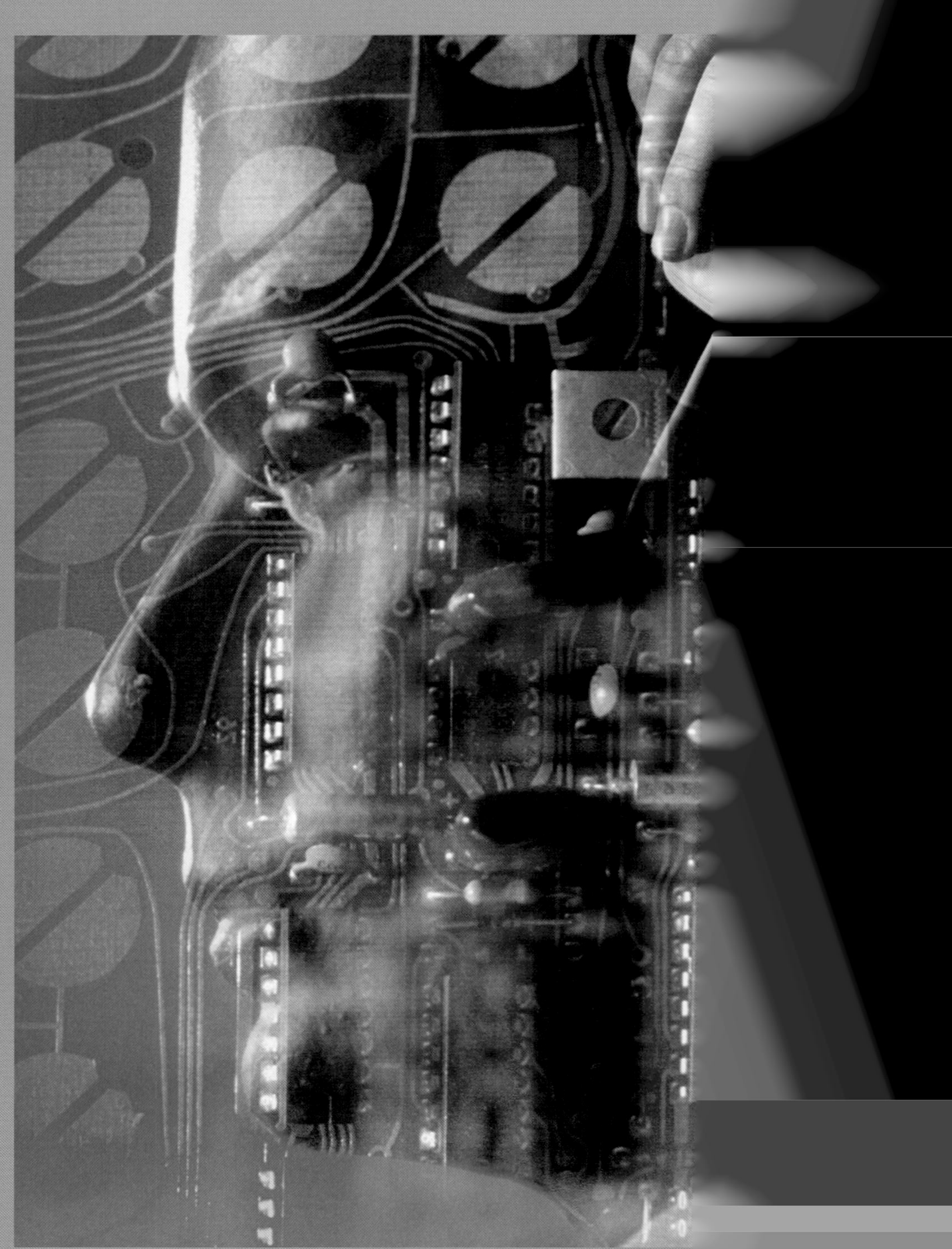

The computer world contains a shadowy realm of h
their knowledge of programming to commit crimes.

SELF-DISCIPLINE AND DILIGENCE

If you give up, you'll never know what you might have accomplished.

CHAPTER SEVEN

Jamie Franklin groaned as he got out of bed. As a member of Canada's national intelligence organization, the CID, he seldom had a chance to sleep late the way he had loved to do when he was back in college. The demands of his job meant constant practice and attention to his skills—so when he wasn't actually solving a crime, he needed to be honing his crime-fighting techniques. That way whenever he needed a specific skill, he could count on it being ready and waiting for use. He didn't ever want to be caught unprepared for his job . . . but he had to admit, he needed plenty of self-discipline and diligence to keep himself motivated—especially at six o'clock in the morning.

People who value self-discipline and diligence:

- work to control their emotions, words, actions, and impulses.
- give their best in all situations.
- keep going even when the going is rough.
- are determined and patient.
- try again even when they fail the first time.
- look for ways to do their work better.

Adapted from material from the Character Education Network (www.CharacterEd.Net).

Jamie was currently in the midst of an investigation. A small group of *hackers* were suspected of doing business in the area. The group consisted of two young adults and three teenagers, and together they had broken into numerous Internet accounts. Even more serious, Jamie suspected they had gained access to an E-mail server on several occasions, retrieving several *encrypted* password files. One of

An investigator will need self-discipline and diligence as he uses the computer to search out criminals.

these files contained several thousand Internet user IDs and passwords for government organizations, private companies, and individual account holders. At this point in the investigation, Jamie had decided the hackers' main motivation was simply the thrill of hacking "secure" electronic sites. They apparently had no particularly sinister use for the information they had obtained.

The investigation had been a long and slow one. Hackers don't usually run around the country with guns; so there had been no high-speed chases, no undercover investigations, no excitement at all. Jamie had used his own considerable computer skills to trace the hackers' trail. Day after day, hour after hour, he had diligently pursued them through the Internet's complex web. Only self-discipline had kept him focused on the investigation.

As the investigation drew to a close at last, Jamie was increasingly concerned he had not reached the bottom of this crime. For instance, he

The Royal Canadian Mounted Police (RCMP) is involved in four levels of policing: international, national, provincial and local. It is criminal intelligence that enables the organization to "connect the dots", in order to increase public safety, i.e. follow manifestations of unlawful activity from 'local to global' to prevent crime and to investigate criminal activity. Intelligence-led policing requires reliance on intelligence before decisions are taken, be they tactical or strategic…Information collected in the context of lawful investigations by the RCMP is collated with information from many other sources. It becomes intelligence when it is analyzed in the Criminal Intelligence Program (CIP) by professional criminal intelligence analysts to ascertain validity and ensure accuracy before it is included in a threat assessment.

From www.rcmp-grc.gc.ca/ci-rc/index-eng.htm

Hackers gain a feeling of power and prestige through invading private computer files. They may think their activity is a joke—but it is really a crime.

According to *Hackers: Crime in the Digital Sublime*, a study by Paul A. Taylor, hackers often belong to a social subculture. Recognition from their peers is a motivating factor behind hacking. They often belong to a social network where they can exchange hacking information—and brag about their own accomplishments. They teach each other how to infiltrate and sometimes vandalize the world's computer systems. As our society depends more and more on computers and the Internet, hacking is an ever-increasing crime—and one whose implications are growing more serious as well.

still did not know how the hackers had gained the information that allowed them to gain access to the E-mail server. He was convinced the techniques the hackers had used showed a level of sophistication that went beyond what he would expect of young adults fooling around. Jamie's *hypothesis* was this: somewhere out there in cyberspace was a hacker mentor, someone who was passing along tools and techniques. A fellow CID investigator had shared with Jamie the fact that another teenage hacker had suddenly seemed to magically transform into a sophisticated hacker over the space of three short

The Canadian Security Intelligence Service (CSIS) is another government agency dedicated to protecting Canada's homeland. The main objective of this agency is to investigate and report on threats to the security of Canada. It is the government's principle advisor on national security.

A hacker who breaks into private computer files is as guilty as the thief who breaks into a home.

weeks. By the time the CID caught up with him, he had gained access to over 100 computer servers in Canada, the United States, and Europe. Jamie wondered if this teenager had hooked up with the same hacker mentor as his group had.

As a CID agent, Jamie could not leap to conclusions. He had to take his time and test each theory carefully. His commanding officer had decided Jamie should put in more hours tracing the hacker group; eventually, he might catch not only a bunch of young adults, but the more dangerous force behind them.

Sometimes Jamie would have liked to move on to another case. But he knew self-discipline and diligence were vital character qualities for his career. He intended to stick with the investigation until the truth was revealed.

73

A professional is one who does his best when he feels the least like working.

—Frank Lloyd Wright

Cute little terriers like this one help a member of the National Guard to give something back to her community.

CITIZENSHIP

Like wild geese flying in V-formation, together we can do more.

CHAPTER EIGHT

Sergeant Noralee Perkins loves dogs. She also loves working with people. Although her life is busy, filled with both family and her work as a National Guard, Noralee makes time to reach out to others. And she's found a way she can use her love of dogs to help those who are sick and discouraged.

It all started back in 1990, when she began volunteering at a local humane society. A program started there that arranged for the shelter's dogs to visit patients in an *Alzheimer's* ward. According to Therapy Dogs International (TDI), when patients are allowed to interact with dogs, the patients' blood pressure, stress levels, and depression all decrease. After her experiences with the humane society, Noralee was hooked.

Being a person of character means you choose to do the right thing at home, at work, and in the community. It is a balancing act of being simultaneously trusting, respectful, responsible, fair and caring while being a good citizen, says Michael Josephson, the founder of the Josephson Institute of Ethics in Marina del Rey. At its most difficult, Josephson warns, being ethical means making choices that may cost money, a job, or a friend. "The wonderful thing about ethics is it's purely about choices," Josephson said. "You can be a horrible person yesterday and a better person today."

When Noralee got a Cairn terrier named Snickers, she knew the little dog had the right temperament to be a "puppy physician." Snickers was calm and gentle, just right for working with patients. Noralee got Snickers certified through TDI, and they began visiting patients in and around Jacksonville, Arkansas. Soon she added two other dogs to her team—Bisquit and Abby. She called her volunteer work "Heavenly Hounds."

Eventually, Noralee decided to get more people involved, and she organized a local TDI chapter. The group has grown to 14 members and 17 dogs. In one year alone, Noralee visited about 40 patients with her dogs, and she traveled 1,600 miles to various hospitals. She told Staff Sergeant Bob Oldham, National Guard's 189th Airlift Wing Public Affairs Officer, "It is so gratifying to see your dog connecting with someone. You work just to see the smiles and the enjoyment as folks pet your dog."

The National Guard recognized Noralee Perkins' citizenship. She recently received the Military Outstanding Volunteer Service Medal for her work with Heavenly Hounds.

Some people put in a day's work and then go home. They never find the time to reach out beyond themselves. But good citizens like Noralee Perkins use all the other core character qualities for the good of the community. With integrity, compassion, justice, responsibility, courage, and self-discipline, they reach out in any way they

People who value citizenship:

- play by the rules.
- obey the law.
- do their share.
- respect authority.
- stay informed about current events.
- vote.
- protect their neighbors and community.
- pay their taxes.
- give to others in their community who are in need.
- volunteer to help.
- protect the environment.
- conserve natural resources for the future.

Adapted from material from the Character Counts Coalition, charactercounts.org/overview/about.html.

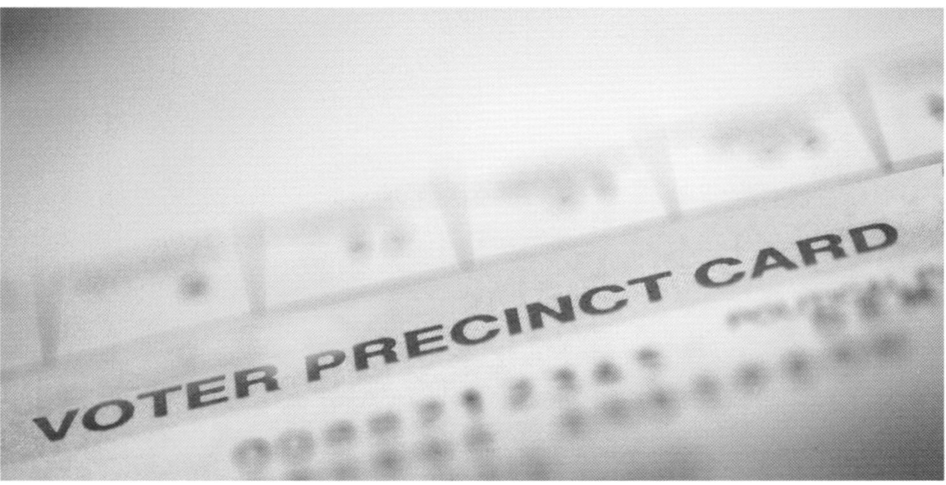

Voting is one way to be a good citizen.

Noralee Perkins isn't the only member of the National Guard that works hard for her community. Fifty members of the Delaware Air National Guard unit spent a weekend helping to build a playground at an elementary school. They were proud to give something back to their community by helping it become a better place for its youngest members. When the playground project was complete, students from the elementary school sent a giant thank-you card. The National Guard members kept it on display at their headquarters.

can to help those around them.

As human beings, we're a little like the geese you sometimes see flying overhead in V-formation in the fall or spring: because they work together, those geese fly faster and farther. In fact, scientists have determined that because the flock flies in formation, they can fly 71 percent farther than if each bird flew alone. That's because when each goose flaps its wings, it creates an updraft for the goose

National Guard members who help build a playground for children are working hard for their community.

The National Guard also has an Air branch.

The National Guard has an Army branch and an Air branch. According to the Air National Guard's web site, "Air National Guard members take pride in being active role models for their communities. During times of celebration or trouble, the Air National Guard provides resources and support needed to get the job done. We have helped with such projects as Habitat for Humanity and Red Cross blood drives. We have supported our communities with time, sweat, and supplies during hurricanes, tornados, and earthquakes. As an institution, the Air National Guard is committed to the vision of being a mirror of the people and values of America."

FBI officers also reach out to their communities. For instance, the FBI has created the Adopt-A-School program, which teaches crime prevention techniques in elementary, middle, and high schools nationwide. The Junior Special Agent program is a part of this. This program focuses on fifth and sixth graders who may be at risk of becoming involved in crime. The program offers students incentives to improve school attendance, academic achievement, and behavior—and FBI agents provide role models that carry an anti-drug, anti-gang, and anti-violence message. The kids in the program get an inside look at the FBI, and they participate in a wide range of activities, including field trips and exercise. The agents involved in this program are good citizens who are making an important contribution to communities across the country.

behind it. As the lead goose gets tired, it falls back and lets someone else take over the leadership role. Meanwhile, the geese in back honk encouragement to those out in front. If a goose does drop out of the V, it feels the wind resistance and quickly gets back into formation. The geese even look out for each other when they're sick or wounded: two geese always follow an injured bird who drops down to the ground, and they stay with it until it either heals or dies.

Some people live their lives according to the philosophy, "Every man for himself." They pursue their own career goals and don't get involved with the community that lies beyond their homes and jobs. But like wild geese, human beings can accomplish so much more when they work together. We all depend on one another–and citizenship is the formation that helps us all work together.

Alone we can do so little; together we can do so much.

—Helen Keller

Homeland security officers must be prepared to deal with a variety of dangerous situations.

CAREER OPPORTUNITIES

The opportunity to do good is worth as much as any paycheck.

CHAPTER NINE

Lisa Jackson's stomach was full of butterflies. You'd never know from watching her, though, that she wasn't a street-hardened junkie. As an undercover DEA agent, she was getting ready to buy cocaine from a suspected dealer. As soon as Lisa exchanged the money for the drugs, she signaled to her backup agents. They rushed in and made the arrest—and within a few minutes, they were reading the dealer his rights. Lisa let out a long sigh of relief. Everything had gone smoothly, this time around. She smiled, experiencing the adrenaline rush that was part of the reason why she loved her job.

The jobs of some federal agents, like the Secret Service and DEA special agents, require plenty of travel, often on very short notice. They may also be asked to relocate several times over the course of their careers.

Homeland security officers like Lisa do have jobs with many opportunities for excitement. They also encounter numerous other opportunities—both professional and personal—in the course of their professional careers.

One way to reach some of the professional opportunities is

Drug traffic is an ongoing problem for homeland security officers.

Here are the number of hours worked by sheriffs and deputy sheriffs:

3.28% (0-20 Hours)
0.98% (21-34 Hours)
0.65% (35-39 Hours)
74.42% (40 Hours)
9.12% (41-49 Hours)
11.55% (Over 50 Hours)

From www.myfuture.com/careers/details/sheriffs-and-deputy-sheriffs_33-3051.03

through ongoing training. Police department academies and state and federal training centers for public safety employees provide programs in self-defense tactics, firearms, use-of-force policies, sensitivity and communication skills, crowd-control techniques, relevant legal developments, and advances in law enforcement equipment. Many agencies will also pay all or at least part of the tuition for officers to work toward degrees in criminal justice, police science, administration of justice, or public administration. Officers with this additional training receive higher salaries.

Overall employment of homeland security officers is expected to keep increasing–and at a faster rate than will most occupations. We

Some officers, like the U.S. Border Patrol, spend most of their time outdoors. This means they must be prepared for all kinds of weather conditions—but it also means they have the ideal job for people who get restless sitting in an office behind a desk.

Michigan State Police Code of Ethics

As a law enforcement officer, my fundamental duty is to serve the community; to safeguard lives and property; to protect the innocent against deception, the weak against oppression or intimidation and the peaceful against violence, or disorder; and to respect the constitutional rights of all to liberty, equality, and justice.

I will keep my private life unsullied as an example to all and will behave in a manner that does not bring discredit to me or my agency. I will maintain courageous calm in the face of danger, scorn, or ridicule; develop self-restraint; and be constantly mindful of the welfare of others. Honest in thought and deed in both my personal and official life, I will be exemplary in obeying the law and the regulations of my department. Whatever I see or hear of a confidential nature or that is confided to me in my official capacity will be kept ever secret unless revelation is necessary in the performance of my duty.

I will never act officiously or permit personal feelings, prejudices, political beliefs, aspirations, animosities, or friendships to influence my decisions. With no compromise for crime and with relentless prosecution of criminals, I will enforce the law courteously and appropriately without fear or favor, malice, or ill will, never employing unnecessary force or violence and never accepting gratuities.

live in a dangerous world, and as people become increasingly aware of the world's dangers, the demand for these officers will increase as well. Drugs are another factor in our society that also means there will be increasing numbers of jobs in the field of law enforcement. Local and state departments will likely have more openings—but at the federal level, budget constraints may limit law enforcement agencies' hiring. However, trained law enforcement officers who lose their jobs because of budget cuts usually have little problem

I recognize the badge of my office as a symbol of public faith, and I accept it as a public trust to be held so long as I am true to the ethics of police service. I will never engage in acts of corruption or bribery, nor will I condone such acts by other police officers. I will cooperate with all legally authorized agencies and their representatives in the pursuit of justice.

I know that I alone am responsible for my own standard of professional performance and will take every reasonable opportunity to enhance and improve my level of knowledge and competence.

I will constantly strive to achieve these objectives and ideals, dedicating myself before God to my chosen profession—law enforcement.

finding jobs with other agencies. As workers retire, they will create job openings as well. Some professionals in this field also "burn out" from the stress; as they transfer to other careers, they leave openings that new recruits can fill.

Departments understand that homeland security can be a stressful field, and they try to compensate workers accordingly. For instance, federal law provides special salary rates to federal employees who serve in law enforcement positions. Federal special agents and inspectors also receive law enforcement availability pay (LEAP) because of the large amount of overtime these agents are expected to work. LEAP can equal up to 25 percent of the agent's regular annual salary. This means that in the year 2011 some FBI agents received a base annual salary of nearly $50,000—but with LEAP earnings, they received nearly $62,500 that year. By the same token, FBI agents in supervisory or management positions had a

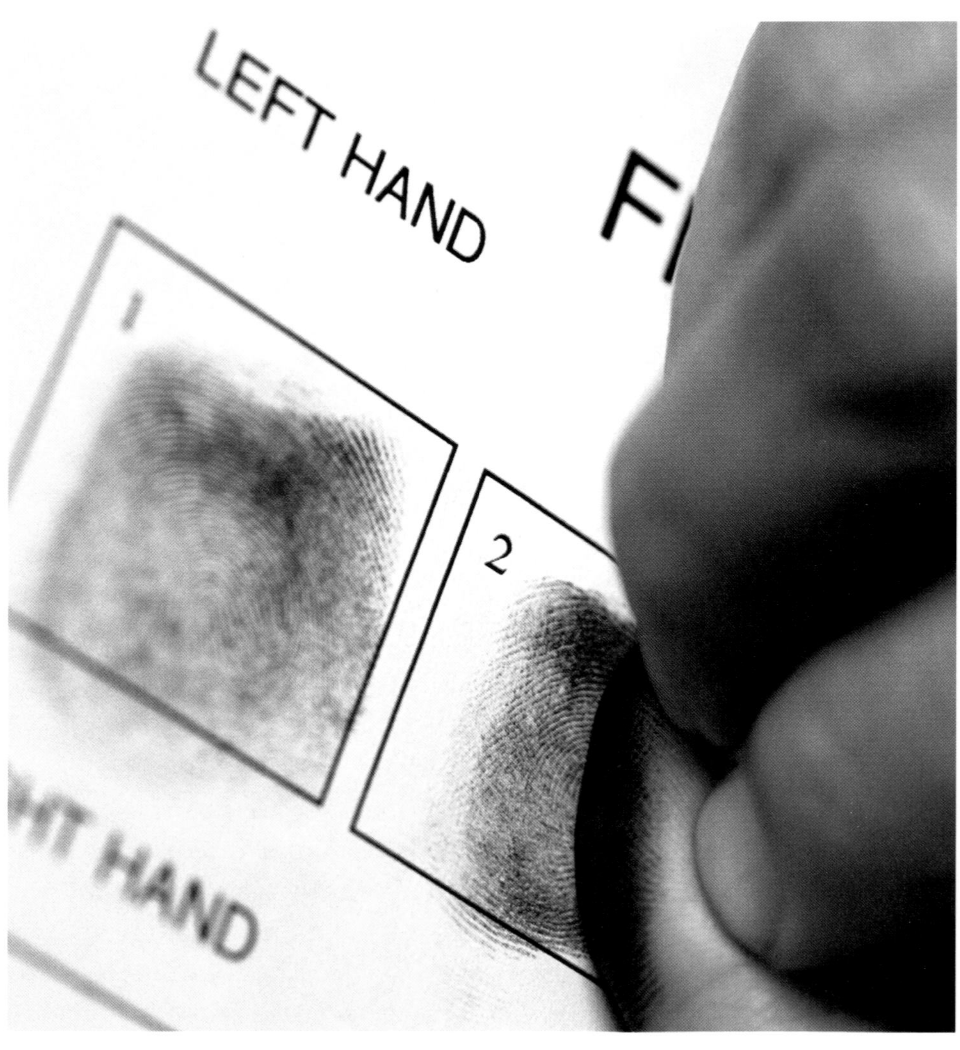

Fingerprinting allows homeland security officers a way to track criminals.

pay base between $84,000 and $130,000 a year—but received between $105,000 and $162,500 because of LEAP. At the state and local levels as well, overtime payments pad officers' salary packages significantly. Federal agents may also be eligible for special law enforcement benefits packages.

One significant opportunity offered by a career in homeland security is the chance to retire early. Most police officers are covered by liberal pension plans that mean they can retire at half-pay after 20 or 25 years of service. This means that if you choose one of these careers, you will have the opportunity to pursue a second career while you are still in your 40s.

Because of these relatively attractive salaries and benefits, the number of qualified candidates is greater than the number of job openings in federal law enforcement agencies, and in most state and local departments as well. As a result, employers in this field have raised their hiring standards. They are increasingly picky about choosing applicants, and their decisions are based on education, experience, and character. You may be more apt to gain experience in a smaller rural department or an urban community where the salaries are lower (and the crime rates may be higher). Applicants who have college training in police science, military police experience, or both will find the best opportunities.

Most important, however, homeland security jobs offer the chance to serve your community, whether at the local, state, or national level. The job is challenging—but with the core qualities of a good character, you can truly make a difference.

As a homeland security officer, you will have opportunities to:

- demonstrate your integrity and trustworthiness.
- treat others with respect and compassion.
- show justice and fairness in all you do.

- act responsibly.
- face danger with courage.
- be self-disciplined and diligent enough to keep trying and never give up.
- make a difference in your community through practicing good citizenship.

Remember, good character is a choice.
What do you choose?

I want you to start a crusade in your life—to dare be your best.
—William Danworth

Further Reading

Ackerman, Thomas H. FBI Careers: *The Ultimate Guide to Landing a Job as One of America's Finest*. Indianapolis, Ind.: JIST Publishing, 2006.

Department of the Defense. *21st Century Complete Guide to the U.S. Coast Guard: Current Events, News, Homeland Security, Immigration, Vessels, Aircraft, Lighthouses, Polar Icebreaking, History, at War, and Safety*. Washington, D.C.: Department of the Defense, 2002.

Josephson, Michael S. and Wes Hanson, editors. *The Power of Character*. Bloomington, Ind.: Unlimited Press, 2004.

Kidder, Rushworth M. *How Good People Make Tough Choices*. New York: HarperCollins, 2009.

LearningExpress Editors. *Becoming a Homeland Security Professional*. New York: LearningExpress, 2010.

Vise, David A. *The Bureau and the Mole: The Unmasking of Robert Hanssen, the Most Dangerous Double Agent in FBI History*. Boston: Atlantic Monthly Press, 2001.

For More Information

Canadian Security Intelligence Service
www.csis-scrs.gc.ca

Center for the 4th and 5th Rs
www.cortland.edu/c4n5rs

Character Education Network
www.charactered.net

Federal Bureau of Investigation
www.fbi.gov

Josephson Institute of Ethics
www.josephsoninstitute.org

Office of Homeland Security
www.whitehouse.gov/homeland

Royal Canadian Mounted Police
www.rcmp-grc.gc.ca/index.htm

United States Coast Guard
www.uscg.mil

Publisher's Note:
The websites on this page were active at the time of publication. The publisher is not responsible for websites that have changed their address or discontinued operation since the date of publication. The publisher will review and update the websites upon each reprint.

Glossary

Alzheimer's A degenerative disease of the central nervous system causing mental deterioration.

Copyright infringement When someone publishes, reproduces, or sells material where the exclusive legal rights have been granted to someone else.

Counterintelligence Activity intended to block an enemy's sources of information, deceive an enemy, prevent sabotage, and gather military and political information.

Covert Hidden, secret.

Drug trafficking The business of buying and selling drugs.

Encrypted Written in a secret code.

Ethical Having to do with decisions about right and wrong.

Extortion Obtaining funds or something else of value through force, intimidation, or an illegal use of political power.

Forensic Having to do with applying scientific knowledge to legal problems.

Hackers People who illegally gain access to and sometimes tamper with computer systems.

Hypothesis An educated guess or theory.

Jurisdiction Having the authority to apply laws.

KGB The police force in charge of internal security within the old Soviet government.

Money laundering Transferring illegally obtained funds through an outside party to conceal the true source.

Recruits New members.

White-collar crime Illegal activities committed by salaried professionals.

Wiretaps Tapping a telephone line to listen and get information.

Index

About the Author & Consultants

Ellyn Sanna has authored more than 50 books, including adult nonfiction, novels, young adult biographies, and gift books.

Cheryl Gholar is a Community and Economic Development Educator with the University of Illinois Extension. She has a Ph.D. in Educational Leadership and Policy Studies from Loyola University, and she has more than 20 years of experience with the Chicago Public Schools as a teacher, counselor, guidance coordinator, and administrator. Recognized for her expertise in the field of character education, Dr. Gholar assisted in developing the K–12 Character Education Curriculum for the Chicago Public Schools, and she is a five-year participant in the White House Conference on Character Building for a Democratic and Civil Society. The recipient of numerous awards, she is also the author of *Beyond Rhetric and Rainbows: A Journey to the Place Where Learning Lives.*

Ernestine G. Riggs is an Assistant Professor at Loyola University Chicago and a Senior Program Consultant for the North Central Regional Educational Laboratory. She has a Ph.D. in Educational Leadership and Policy Studies from Loyola University, and she has been involved in the field of education for more than 35 years. An advocate of teaching the whole child, she is a frequent presenter at district and national conferences; she also serves as a consultant for several state boards of education. Dr. Riggs has received many citations, including an award from the United States Department of Defense Overseas Schools for Outstanding Elementary Teacher of America.